Rookie Read-About™ Science

Frogs and Toads and Tadpoles, Too

By Allan Fowler

Consultants:

Robert L. Hillerich, Ph.D., Bowling Green State University, Bowling Green, Ohio

Mary Nalbandian, Director of Science, Chicago Public Schools, Chicago, Illinois

Fay Robinson, Child Development Specialist

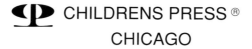

CHILDRENS PRESS ®

CHICAGO

Design by Beth Herman Design Associates

Library of Congress Cataloging-in-Publication Data

Fowler, Allan
Frogs and Toads, and tadpoles too! / by Allan Fowler.
     p. cm. – (Rookie read-about science)
    Summary: Explains basic likenesses and differences about frogs and toads.
    ISBN 0-516-04925-9
    1.Frogs– Juvenile literature.. 2. Toads– Juvenile literature.
3. Tadpoles– Juvenile literature.
    [1. Frogs. 2. Toads.] I. Title. II. Series: Fowler, Allan.
    Rookie read-about science.
QLL668.06F68 1992
597.8–dc20   91-42178
                                                CIP
                                               AC

Look at this bullfrog croaking!

4

Most male frogs and
toads puff up their
throats when they make
a sound.

Not all frogs and
toads make the same
sound.

There are little tree frogs,
called spring peepers,
that peep.

In Texas, there are frogs
that bark like dogs.

The green frog makes a
twanging sound like the
bass string of a banjo.

Frogs and toads are amphibians. That means they live both on land and in water.

Frogs are usually found
around marshes, ponds,
or other wet places.

Toads live mostly on
dry land.

13

Frogs have shiny, smooth
skin.

Toads have rough, bumpy skin.

Both are often brownish
or dark green in color,

with stripes or markings
in other colors.

But some frogs are bright
green, blue, white,
yellow, or red.

Frogs can jump farther than toads.

Many frogs have webbed
feet that help them swim.

Tree frogs have special
pads on their toes that
help them climb.

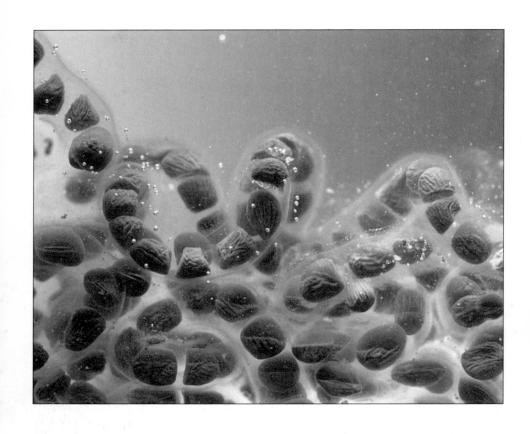

Most toads and frogs lay
their eggs in water, where
the eggs hatch into tadpoles.

A tadpole looks like a fish.
It has gills for breathing
under the water and a tail.

After a while, the
tadpole begins to grow
legs and to lose its tail.
Its gills are replaced by
lungs and it can breathe
air just like you do.
It can live out of water.

It can shoot out its long, sticky tongue and catch insects to eat.

Now it's a toad or a frog!

Words You Know

frog

bullfrog

spring peeper

toad

webbed feet

30

frog eggs   tadpole

amphibians

Index

amphibians, 10
banjo, 9
bark, 8
bullfrog, 3
climb, 23
color, 16, 17, 19
croaking, 3, 7
eggs, 24
feet, 22
fish, 25
frogs, 3, 5, 7 , 8, 9, 10, 12, 14, 19, 20, 23, 24, 29
gills, 25, 26
green frog, 9
insects, 29
jump, 20
land, 10, 13
legs, 26
lungs, 26
male frogs and toads, 5
markings, 17
marshes, 12
pads, 23
ponds, 12
skin, 14, 15
sounds, 5, 7, 8
spring peepers, 7
swim, 22
tadpoles, 24, 25, 26
tail, 25, 26
Texas, 8
throats, 5
toads, 5, 7, 10, 13, 15, 20, 24, 29
toes, 23
tongue, 29
tree frogs, 7, 23
water, 10, 24, 26
webbed feet, 22

About the Author

Allan Fowler is a free-lance writer with a background in advertising. Born in New York, he lives in Chicago now and enjoys traveling.

Photo Credits

Animals Animals - ©Stephen Dalton, 21, 28

Valan - ©Albert Kuhnigk, Cover, 16; 23 ©Stephen Krasemann, 3, 14, 18, 30 (top right); ©Robert C. Simpson, 6, 30 (center right); ©Jim Merli, 4, 8, 17, 30 (top left); ©John Fowler, 9; ©Pam Hickman, 11; ©J. A. Wilkinson, 12, 22, 25, 30 (bottom right), 31 (top right and bottom left); ©Dennis W. Schmidt, 13, 31 (bottom right); ©John Cancalosi, 15, 27, 30 (bottom left); ©Harold V. Green, 24, 31 (top left)

COVER: Gray Tree frog